CW01510938

Thank you for purchasir
powerful quotes give you the inspiration you need to
succeed in whatever endeavor you find yourself in the
middle of.

For even more inspiration check out our collection of eye-
catching typography artwork. Our museum-quality posters
and hand-stretched canvas prints make a statement in any
room while featuring one of our hand-picked inspirational
quotes.

www.QuotesThatInspire.me

You are never too old
to set another goal
or dream a new dream

–C.S Lewis

~

Success is falling nine times
and getting up ten

–Jon Bon Jovi

If you really want to do something, you'll find a way. If you don't, you'll find an excuse

–Jim Rohn

~

It's not the years in your life that count. It's the life in your years

–Abraham Lincoln

Do one thing every day that scares you

scares you

–Eleanor Roosevelt

~

Twenty years from now you will be more disappointed by the things that you didn't do than by the ones you did do, so throw off the bowlines, sail away from safe harbor, catch the trade winds in your sails. Explore, Dream, Discover

–Mark Twain

Live as if you were to die tomorrow. Learn as if you were to live forever

-Mahatma Gandhi

~

The question isn't who is going to let me; it's who is going to stop me

-Ayn Rand

Don't worry about failures, worry about the chances you miss when you don't even try

—Jack Canfield

~

Overcome the notion that you must be regular. It robs you of the chance to be extraordinary

–Uta Hagen

NEVER, EVER EVER EVER EVER GIVE UP

WINSTON CHURCHILL

~

There are two ways to live: you can live as if nothing is a miracle; you can live as if everything is a miracle

-Albert Einstein

Life is not measured by
the number of breaths
we take, but by the
moments that take our
breath away

–Maya Angelou

~

I would rather die of
passion than of
boredom

–Vincent van Gogh

A buoyant- positive approach to the game is as basic as a sound swing.

-Tony Lema

~

In life you need either inspiration or desperation.

-Tony Robbins

Life changes when you start
taking a comment as a
compliment.

-Author Unknown

~

He who lives in
harmony with himself
lives in harmony with
the universe.

-Marcus Aurelius

Don't go around saying the world owes you a living. The world owes you nothing. It was here first.

Mark Twain

~

Ideas can be life-changing. Sometimes all you need to open the door is just one more good idea.

-Jim Rohn

Learn to appreciate
what you have and
where and who you
are.

-Wayne Dyer

~

**Better understated than
overstated. Let people be
surprised that it was more than
you promised & easier than you
said.**

-Jim Rohn

Go to Heaven for the climate, Hell for the company.

Mark Twain

~

I often try to tell kids to think about all the people who love you- don't cry over the one person who doesn't.

-Bill Cosby

No man has a good enough memory to be a successful liar.

-Abraham Lincoln

~

It is in men as in soils where sometimes there is a vein of gold which the owner knows not.

-Jonathan Swift

How am I going to live today in order to create the tomorrow I'm committed to?

-Tony Robbins

~

EVERY OBNOXIOUS ACT IS A CRY FOR HELP.

-ZIG ZIGLAR

May you live all the days of your life.

-Jonathan Swift

~

I walk slowly – but I never walk backward.

-Abraham Lincoln

Go for it now. The future is promised to no one.

–Wayne Dyer

~

Remember that failure is an event- not a person.

-Zig Ziglar

Anything you really
want- you can attain-
if you really go
after it.

-Wayne Dyer

~

**A wise man should have
money in his head- but not in
his heart.**

-Jonathan Swift

Live one day at a time emphasizing ethics rather than rules.

-Wayne Dyer

~

Improve your business- your life- your relationships- your finances & your health. When you do the whole world improves.

-Mark Victor Hansen

I think anytime you can affect people in general- in a positive way- then you're a lucky individual.

-Sam Elliott

~

Age is an issue of mind over matter. If you don't mind, it doesn't matter.

Mark Twain

Doing what you love is the cornerstone of having abundance in your life.

-Wayne Dyer

~

The discipline of desire is the background of character.

-John Locke

The greatest mistake we make
is living in constant fear that
we will make one.

-John Maxwell

~

**Anger is an acid that can do more harm to the vessel in which it is stored than to anything on which it is poured.
Mark Twain**

Other people's opinion of you does not have to become your reality.

-Les Brown

~

Passion plus inspiration leads to fulfillment.

-Sheye Hassan

BEGIN TO SEE YOURSELF AS A SOUL WITH A BODY RATHER THAN A BODY WITH A SOUL.

-WAYNE DYER

~

It is better to remain silent and be thought a fool than to open one's mouth and remove all doubt.

Mark Twain

The foundation stones for a balanced success are honesty- character- integrity- faith- love & loyalty.

-Zig Ziglar

~

Achievement brings its own anticlimax.

-Maya Angelou

Adopting the right attitude
can convert a negative stress
into a positive one.

-Hans Selye

~

If you tell the
truth, you don't have
to remember anything.
Mark Twain

Someone's sitting in the shade today because someone planted a tree a long time ago. Les Brown

~

In life- trying is worth trying.

Larispique Philidor

Accept responsibility for your life. Know that it is you who will get you where you want to go- no one else.

-Les Brown

~

The few who do are the envy of the many who only watch.

-Jim Rohn

Forgive yourself for your faults & your mistakes & move on.

-Les Brown

~

The book you don't read won't help.

-Jim Rohn

Don't ever let economic alone determine your career or how you spend the majority of your time.

-Denis Waitley

~

One enemy can do more hurt than ten friends can do good.

-Jonathan Swift

Kindness is the language which the deaf can hear and the blind can see.

Mark Twain

~

The key to success is to focus our conscious mind on things we desire not things we fear.

Brian Tracy

Everybody likes a
compliment.

-Abraham Lincoln

~

I AM A POSITIVE PERSON. I NEVER THINK
OF THE GLASS AS HALF EMPTY. I JUST
KEEP PUSHING FORWARD.

-ROSIE PEREZ

The fear of death follows from the fear of life. A man who lives fully is prepared to die at any time.

Mark Twain

~

Maturity is the ability to reap without apology & not complain when things don't go well.

–Jim Rohn

Real magic in relationships means an absence of judgment of others.

-Wayne Dyer

~

Remember- a real decision is measured by the fact that you've taken new action. If there's no action- you haven't truly decided.

-Tony Robbins

To succeed in life,
you need two things:
ignorance and
confidence.

Mark Twain

~

Goals help you channel your energy into action.

-Les Brown

Live a life as a
monument to your
soul.

-Ayn Rand

~

Art is not a study of positive
reality- it is the seeking for
ideal truth.

-John Ruskin

A man is never more truthful than when he acknowledges himself a liar.

Mark Twain

~

Some day I shall be President.

-Abraham Lincoln

I surround myself with positive-productive people of good will & decency.

-Ted Nugent

~

Never say anything about yourself you do not want to come true.

-Brian Tracy

The secret of getting ahead is getting started.

Mark Twain

~

It doesn't matter where you are coming from. All that matters is where you are going.

-Brian Tracy

Every choice you make has an end result.

-Zig Ziglar

~

Leaders are readers.

-Charles Tremendous Jones

SUCCESS IS DEPENDENT UPON THE
GLANDS – SWEAT GLANDS.

-ZIG ZIGLAR

~

Be sure you put your feet
in the right place- then
stand firm.

-Abraham Lincoln

Leadership is influence.

–John Maxwell

~

In order to carry a positive action we must develop here a positive vision.

–Dalai Lama

The best way to cheer yourself up is to try to cheer somebody else up.

Mark Twain

~

I want to talk with people who care about things that matter that will make a life-changing difference.

-Mark Victor Hansen

Honor your commitments with integrity.

-Les Brown

~

He who is not courageous enough to take risks will accomplish nothing in life.

-Muhammad Ali

Effective communication is 20% what you know and 80% how you feel about what you know.

-Jim Rohn

~

The best thing about the future is that it comes one day at a time.

-Abraham Lincoln

Do the right thing.
It will gratify some
people and astonish
the rest.

Mark Twain

~

**In imagination- there's no
limitation.**

-Mark Victor Hansen

Life has no limitations-
except the ones you
make.

-Les Brown

~

If it ain't fun don't do it.

-Jack Canfield

A risk-free life is far from being a healthy life.

-Deepak Chopra

~

Make measurable progress in reasonable time.

-Jim Rohn

I like to encourage people to realize that any action is a good action if it's proactive & there is positive intent behind it.

Michael J. Fox

~

A MAN'S CHARACTER MAY BE LEARNED FROM THE ADJECTIVES WHICH HE HABITUALLY USES IN CONVERSATION.

MARK TWAIN

No one is a failure until they blame somebody else.

-Charles Tremendous Jones

~

Educators take something simple & make it complicated. Communicators take something complicated & make it simple.

-John Maxwell

It is not in the pursuit of happiness that we find fulfillment- it is in the happiness of pursuit.

-Denis Waitley

~

Live with passion!

-Tony Robbins

People have to remain
positive & believe in
those dreams. It's
really important.

-Kirsty Coventry

~

**Only the insecure strive for
security.**

-Wayne Dyer

Affirmation without discipline is the beginning of delusion.

-Jim Rohn

~

It's not the size of the dog in the fight, it's the size of the fight in the dog.

Mark Twain

I never had a policy; I have just tried to do my very best each & every day.

-Abraham Lincoln

~

In order to succeed-
your desire for
success should be
greater than your
fear of failure.

-Bill Cosby

Give me six hours to chop down a tree & I will spend the first four sharpening the axe.

Abraham Lincoln

~

Be miserable. Or motivate yourself. Whatever has to be done- it's always your choice.

-Wayne Dyer

Am I not destroying my
enemies when I make friends
of them?

-Abraham Lincoln

~

**Determination gives you the
resolve to keep going in spite of
the roadblocks that lay before
you.**

-Denis Waitley

The first step is you have to say that you can.

-Will Smith

~

The greatest gift that you can give to others is the gift of unconditional love & acceptance.

-Brian Tracy

OUR JOB IS NOT TO FIGURE OUT THE 'HOW'. THE 'HOW' WILL SHOW UP OUT OF THE COMMITMENT AND BELIEF IN THE 'WHAT.

-JACK CANFIELD

~

Everything is something you decide to do, and there is nothing you have to do.

-Denis Waitley

Life is a game. You win sometimes while other times you lose– then what? Play again.

–Dr. NK Grover

~

Abundance is not something we acquire. It is something we tune into.

–Wayne Dyer

A man cannot be comfortable without his own approval.
Mark Twain

~

All great achievements require time.

-Maya Angelou

Silence is golden when you can't think of a good answer.

-Muhammad Ali

~

Sometimes breakdowns are so important in your life that you come to know your hidden potentials.

-Author Unknown

Shoot for the moon & if you miss you will still be among the stars.

-Les Brown

~

All of us- at certain moments of our lives- need to take advice & to receive help from other people.

-Alexis Carrel

Loving people live in
a loving world.
Hostile people live
in a hostile world.
Same world.

-Wayne Dyer

~

The proper words in the proper
places are the true definition of
style.

-Jonathan Swift

Good executives never
put off until tomorrow what
they can get someone
else to do today.

-John Maxwell

~

Once you replace negative
thoughts with positive ones-
you'll start having positive
results.

-Willie Nelson

Fortitude is the guard & support of the other virtues.

-John Locke

~

Keep your eyes open to your mercies. The man who forgets to be thankful has fallen asleep in life.

-Robert Louis Stevenson

If you have only one smile
in you give it to the people
you love.

-Maya Angelou

~

START EARLY & BEGIN RAISING THE BAR

THROUGHOUT THE DAY.

-BRUCE JENNER

Life loves to be taken by the lapel & told: "I'm with you kid. Let's go."

-Maya Angelou

~

The person who knows HOW will always have a job. The person who knows WHY will always be his boss.

-Diane Ravitch

Happiness is not
something you postpone
for the future; it is
something you design
for the present.

–Jim Rohn

~

Education begins the
gentleman- but reading,
good company and reflection
must finish him.

-John Locke

Public behavior is merely private character writ large.

-Stephen Covey

~

I try to stay positive by focusing on how much I'll appreciate my health if I get better.

-Daniel Johns

It was character that got us out of bed- commitment that moved us into action- & discipline that enabled us to follow through.

-Zig Ziglar

~

A person is a pattern of behavior.

-Deepak Chopra

Life is not a matter of holding good cards- but of playing a poor hand well.

-Robert Louis Stevenson

~

My mom was always the support. I can always go out to her and she'll always find the positive in things

-Caroline Wozniacki

That man is a success who has lived well- laughed often and loved much.

-Robert Louis Stevenson

~

I want the world to be better because I was here.

-Will Smith

Reject your sense of injury &
the injury itself disappears.

-Marcus Aurelius

~

People who have good relationships at home are more effective.

-Zig Ziglar

One characteristic of winners is they always look upon themselves as a do it yourself project.

-Denis Waitley

~

Learn to say 'no' to the good so you can say 'yes' to the best.

-John Maxwell

LOSERS MAKE PROMISES THEY OFTEN
BREAK. WINNERS MAKE COMMITMENTS
THEY ALWAYS KEEP.

-DENIS WATTLEY

~

Life is lived on the edge.

-Will Smith

Happiness is that state of consciousness which proceeds from the achievement of one's values.

-Ayn Rand

Forget about the consequences of failure. Failure is only a temporary change in direction to set you straight for your next success.

-Denis Waitley

Invest in yourself (self-development) in order to guarantee your future.

-Brian Tracy

~

Always bear in mind that your own resolution to succeed is more important than any other.

-Abraham Lincoln

I have always thought the actions of men the best interpreters of their thoughts.

-John Locke

~

It is the set of the sails- not the direction of the wind that determines which way we will go.

-Jim Rohn

Nothing made by brute force lasts.

-Robert Louis Stevenson

~

Each day provides its own gifts.
-Marcus Aurelius

It is not what we get- but who we become- what we contribute- that gives meaning to our lives.

-Tony Robbins

~

Do the thing you fear most and the death of fear is certain.

Mark Twain

Expect the best- plan for the worst- & prepare to be surprised.

-Denis Waitley

~

I cannot always control what goes on outside. But I can always control what goes on inside.

-Wayne Dyer

As a man is- so he sees. As the eye is formed- such are its powers.

-William Blake

~

If they can make penicillin out of moldy bread- they can sure make something out of you.

-Muhammad Ali

Spread love everywhere you go. Let no one ever come to you without leaving happier.

Mother Teresa

~

SELF-WORTH COMES FROM ONE THING - THINKING THAT YOU ARE WORTHY.

-WAYNE DYER

Always go with your
passions. Never ask yourself
if it's realistic or not.

-Deepak Chopra

~

Practice random acts of
kindness & senseless acts
of beauty.

-Jack Canfield

Self-awareness is value-free. It isn't scary. It doesn't imply that you will subject yourself to needless pain.

-Deepak Chopra

~

Life is not accumulation- it is about contribution.

-Stephen Covey

No bird soars too
high if he soars with
his own wings.

-William Blake

~

**How people treat you is their
karma; how you react is yours.**

-Wayne Dyer

The first time you say something- it's heard. The second time- it's recognized- & the third time it's learned.

-John Maxwell

~

The future is here. It's just not widely distributed yet.

-William Gibson

A good objective of leadership is to help those who are doing poorly to do well & to help those who are doing well to do even better.

-Jim Rohn

~

I've never really viewed myself as particularly talented.

-Will Smith

Successful people ask better questions and as a result- they get better answers.

-Tony Robbins

~

If you can't be happy where you are, you can't be happy where you ain't.

-Charles Tremendous Jones

Forgive those who have hurt you.

-Les Brown

~

Discipline is the bridge between goals & accomplishment.

-Jim Rohn

All wealth is the product of labor.

-John Locke

~

Setting goals is the first step in turning the invisible into the visible.

-Tony Robbins

GIVE WHATEVER YOU ARE DOING &
WHOEVER YOU ARE WITH THE GIFT OF
YOUR ATTENTION.

-JIM ROHN

~

Delete the negative;
accentuate the positive!

-Donna Karan

Don't just read the easy stuff. You may be entertained by it– but you will never grow from it.

–Jim Rohn

~

It's never crowded along the extra mile.

–Wayne Dyer

A lot of people quit looking for work as soon as they find a job.

-Zig Ziglar

~

If you don't like something, change it. If you can't change it, change your attitude.

-Maya Angelou

Take control of your consistent emotions & begin to consciously and deliberately reshape your daily experience of life.

-Tony Robbins

~

A wise man will make more opportunities than he finds.

-Francis Bacon

Happiness is not bought. It is a decision- so decide to be happy today.

-Author Unknown

~

Life is not accountable to us. We are accountable to life.

-Denis Waitley

Remember- man does not live on bread alone: sometimes he needs a little buttering up.

-John Maxwell

~

Policies are many- Principles are few- Policies will change- Principles never do.

-John Maxwell

No wise man ever wished
to be younger.

-Jonathan Swift

~

Live life to the fullest- & focus
on the positive.

-Matt Cameron

I want always to be positive.

-Gianni Versace

~

Invention is the talent of youth- as judgment is of age.

-Jonathan Swift

First of all- I try to be a positive role model.

-Bruce Jenner

~

IT IS EASIER FOR A TUTOR TO COMMAND THAN TO TEACH.

-JOHN LOCKE

An aim in life is the only fortune worth finding.

-Robert Louis Stevenson

~

I figured that if I said it enough– I would convince the world that I really was the greatest.

-Muhammad Ali

Relationships are the hallmark of the mature person.

-Brian Tracy

~

Success comes when people act together; failure tends to happen alone.

-Deepak Chopra

A lot of people do not muster the courage to live their dreams because they are afraid to die.

-Les Brown

~

Better to remain silent & be thought a fool than to speak out & remove all doubt.

-Abraham Lincoln

Everything you want
is out there waiting
for you to ask.
Everything you want
also wants you. But
you have to take
action to get it.

-Jack Canfield

~

Labor gives birth to ideas.

-Jim Rohn

Money won't make you happy... but everybody wants to find out for themselves.

-Zig Ziglar

~

Positive anything is better than negative nothing.

-Elbert Hubbard

Surmounting difficulty is the crucible that forms character.

-Tony Robbins

~

Positive thinking will let you do everything better than negative thinking will.

-Zig Ziglar

Everything you want is on the other side of fear.

-Jack Canfield

~

A strong positive mental attitude will create more miracles than any wonder drug.

-Patricia Neal

Stay committed to your decisions- but stay Flexible in your approach.

-Tony Robbins

~

Don't worry when you are not recognized- but strive to be worthy of recognition.

-Abraham Lincoln

LISTENING IS A POSITIVE ACT: YOU HAVE TO PUT YOURSELF OUT TO DO IT.

-DAVID HOCKNEY

~

The quality of your life is the quality of your relationships.

-Tony Robbins

The gift of fantasy has meant more to me than my talent for absorbing positive knowledge.

– Albert Einstein

~

Our lives are a sum total of the choices we have made.

-Wayne Dyer

Passion is the genesis of genius.

-Tony Robbins

~

Success is doing ordinary things extraordinarily well.

-Jim Rohn

A man must be big enough to admit his mistakes- smart enough to profit from them- & strong enough to correct them.

-John Maxwell

~

Blessed is he who expects nothing- for he shall never be disappointed.

-Jonathan Swift

If you learn from defeat- you haven't really lost.

-Zig Ziglar

~

Lack of forgiveness causes almost all of our self-sabotaging behavior.

-Mark Victor Hansen

More than anything else- I believe it's our decisions- not the conditions of our lives- that determine our destiny.

-Tony Robbins

~

Power is no blessing in itself- except when it is used to protect the innocent.

-Jonathan Swift

It is in your moments of decision that your destiny is shaped.

-Tony Robbins

~

Service to others is the rent you pay for your room here on earth.

-Muhammad Ali

People buy into the leader before they buy into the vision.

-John Maxwell

~

Let fear be a counselor & not a jailer.

-Tony Robbins

Successful people are
always looking for
opportunities to help
others.

-Brian Tracy

~

I DON'T KNOW THE KEY TO SUCCESS- BUT
THE KEY TO FAILURE IS TRYING TO PLEASE
EVERYBODY.

-BILL COSBY

Nearly all men can stand adversity- but if you want to test a man's character- give him power.

-Abraham Lincoln

~

Change the changeable - accept the unchangeable - & remove yourself from the unacceptable

.-Denis Waitley

Love would never be a promise of a rose garden unless it is showered with a light of faith— water of sincerity— & an art of passion.

—Jack Canfield

Mistakes are painful when they happen- but years later a collection of mistakes is what is called experience.

-Denis Waitley

~

People are not lazy. They simply have impotent goals - that is- goals that do not inspire them.

-Tony Robbins

Success is nothing more than a few simple disciplines- practiced every day.

-Jim Rohn

~

A novel is never anything- but a philosophy put into images.

-Jim Rohn

If you want to reach a goal-
you must 'see the reaching' in
your own mind before you
actually arrive at your goal.

-Zig Ziglar

~

*Leaders must be close enough
to relate to others- but far
enough ahead to motivate
them.*

-John Maxwell

Most folks are as happy as they make up their minds to be.

-Abraham Lincoln

~

For every disciplined effort there is a multiple reward.

-Jim Rohn

Judge each day not by the harvest you reap but by the seeds you plant.

-Robert Louis Stevenson

~

In my mind- I've always been an A-list Hollywood superstar. Y'all just didn't know yet.

-Will Smith

I always felt that my greatest asset was not my physical ability- it was my mental ability.

-Bruce Jenner

~

I believe in Karma. If the good is sown- the good is collected. When positive things are made- that returns well.

-Yannick Noah

If what you are doing is not moving you towards your goals- then it's moving you away from your goals.

-Brian Tracy

~

THE PERSON WE BELIEVE OURSELVES TO BE WILL ALWAYS ACT IN A MANNER CONSISTENT WITH OUR SELF-IMAGE.

-BRIAN TRACY

I want my life to effect the balance to the positive.

-Mira Sorvino

~

It's amazing how a competitive nature can turn a negative into something positive.

-Barry Mann

You get treated in life
the way you teach
people to treat you.

-Wayne Dyer

~

Success is steady progress
toward one's personal goals.

-Jim Rohn

I don't know who my grandfather was; I am much more concerned to know what his grandson will be.

-Abraham Lincoln

~

If you're not making mistakes- then you're not doing anything. I'm positive that a doer makes mistakes.

- John Wooden

Learn from the past- set vivid- detailed goals for the future- & live in the only moment of time over which you have any control now.

-Denis Waitley

~

Relentless- repetitive self talk is what changes our self-image.

-Denis Waitley

Happiness is a continuation of happenings which are not resisted.

-Deepak Chopra

~

Everything has positive & negative consequences.

-Farrah Fawcett

A word to the wise ain't necessary - it's the stupid ones that need the advice.

-Bill Cosby

~

Success is not to be pursued; it is to be attracted by the person you become.

-Jim Rohn

Nothing will work unless you do.

-Maya Angelou

~

Design can have such a positive impact on the way people live & on their relationships & moods.

-Genevieve Gorder

Most everything that you want is just outside your comfort zone.

-Jack Canfield

~

Books are good enough in their own way- but they are a poor substitute for life.

-Robert Louis Stevenson

IMPORTANT PRINCIPLES MAY- & MUST-
BE INFLEXIBLE.

-ABRAHAM LINCOLN

~

If you are not willing to risk the unusual- you will have to settle for the ordinary.

-Jim Rohn

It's not the events of our lives that shape us- but our beliefs as to what those events mean.

-Tony Robbins

~

May you have more ambition & determination than you have excuses.

- Robert Moore

People may hear your words-
but they feel your attitude.

-John Maxwell

~

Books serve to show a
man that those
original thoughts of
his aren't very new
at all.

-Abraham Lincoln

Failure is a detour- not a dead- end street.

-Zig Ziglar

~

I'm concentrating on the positive- on all the wonderful things I'm doing now.

-Tia Carrere

It's great to work with somebody who wants to do things differently.

-Author Unknown

~

A man's worth is no greater than his ambitions.

-Marcus Aurelius

So if you stay ready-
you ain't gotta get
ready- & that is how
I run my life.

-Will Smith

~

Our life is what our thoughts make it.

-Marcus Aurelius

Life gives you plenty of time to do whatever you want to do if you stay in the present moment.

-Deepak Chopra

~

If I can inspire someone to go in a positive way & pursue a dream- it can only be good.

-Parminder Nagra

I have to follow my thoughts & mine for the gold. I have to dig it out.

-Bill Cosby

~

I am a positive person & do not allow things to get on top of me.

-Jamie Redknapp

If you change the way you look at things- the things you look at change.

-Wayne Dyer

~

I'VE ALWAYS BELIEVED THAT YOU CAN THINK POSITIVE JUST AS WELL AS YOU CAN THINK NEGATIVE.

-JAMES A. BALDWIN

Miracles come in moments.

Be ready & willing.

-Wayne Dyer

~

A positive attitude can really make dreams come true - it did for me.

-David Bailey

For changes to be of any true value, they've got to be lasting and consistent.

–Tony Robbins

~

I hated every minute of training but I said- 'Don't quit. Suffer now & live the rest of your life as a champion.'

-Muhammad Ali

Giving is better than
receiving because
giving starts the
receiving process.

-Jim Rohn

~

**Personal satisfaction is the
most important ingredient of
success.**

-Denis Waitley

Keep your fears to yourself but share your courage with others.

-Robert Louis Stevenson

~

I'm taking all the negatives in my life- & turning them into a positive.

-Pitbull

I am the greatest- I said that even before I knew I was.

-Muhammad Ali

~

Don't wish it were easier- wish you were better.

-Jim Rohn

Live out of your imagination- not your history.

-Stephen Covey

~

Conflict cannot survive without your participation.

-Wayne Dyer

Money is usually attracted-
not pursued.

-Jim Rohn

~

Frustration- although quite painful at times- is a very positive & essential part of success.

- Bo Bennett

I am more than what I think I can be.
You may be nobody today; tomorrow
you may be somebody.

-Sangeeta Thanainthiram

~

If you don't like how
things are- change it!
You're not a tree.

-Jim Rohn

I'VE TRAINED MYSELF TO ILLUMINATE THE THINGS IN MY PERSONALITY THAT ARE LIKABLE & TO HIDE & PROTECT THE THINGS THAT ARE LESS LIKEABLE.

-WILL SMITH

~

Successful people are simply those with successful habits.

-Brian Tracy

It comes down to building your own world out here on the road. It's who you surround yourself with. My band & crew are really positive.

-Brad Paisley

Having a positive mental attitude is asking how something can be done rather than saying it can't be done.

-Bo Bennett

~

Every closed eye is not sleeping- & every open eye is not seeing.

-Bill Cosby

Achieving the highest possible return on human capital must be every manager's goal.

-Brian Tracy

~

Success is the maximum utilization of the ability that you have.

-Zig Ziglar

I had the blues
because I had no
shoes; until upon the
street I met a man
who had no feet.

-Denis Waitley

~

The probability that we may

fail in the struggle ought not to

deter us from the support of a

cause we believe to be just.

-Abraham Lincoln

I believe in karma- & I believe if you put out positive vibes to everybody- that's all you're going to get back.

-Kesha

~

If you don't see yourself as a winner- then you cannot perform as a winner.

-Zig Ziglar

People who want the most approval get the least & people who need approval the least get the most.

-Wayne Dyer

~

Successful people bring success to what they do.

-Wayne Dyer

A smile is the light in your window that tells others that there is a caring, sharing person inside.

~Denis Waitley

~

Consciousness conceives, governs, constructs, and becomes the activity of the body.

-Deepak Chopra

Reading furnishes the mind only with
materials of knowledge; it is thinking
that makes what we read ours.

-John Locke

~

Failure is simply a few
errors in judgment-
repeated every day.

-Jim Rohn

A POSITIVE ATTITUDE IS SOMETHING
EVERYONE CAN WORK ON- & EVERYONE
CAN LEARN HOW TO EMPLOY IT.

-JOAN LUNDEN

~

Sometimes adversity is
what you need to face in
order to become successful.

-Zig Ziglar

Our character is basically a composite of our habits.

-Stephen Covey

~

Of what shall a man be proud, if he is not proud of his friends?

-Robert Louis Stevenson

Anytime you suffer a setback or disappointment, put your head down and plow ahead.

-Les Brown

~

My great concern is not whether you have failed, but whether you are content with your failure.

-Abraham Lincoln

Books are the children of the brain.

-Jonathan Swift

~

As people are walking all the time in the same spot, a path appears.

-John Locke

A goal properly set is halfway reached.

-Zig Ziglar

~

Be positive in your leadership. Always have a positive approach. This is what will win people

- Anthony Ambrose

Everything is perfect
in the universe, even
your desire to
improve it.

-Wayne Dyer

~

**I believe that every person is born
with talent.**

-Maya Angelou

Miss a meal if you have to,
but don't miss a book.

-Jim Rohn

~

People with clear, written
goals accomplish far more in
a shorter period of time than
people without them could
ever imagine.

-Brian Tracy

Take care of your body. It's the only place you have to live.

-Jim Rohn

~

A strong, positive self-image is the best possible preparation for success.

-Joyce Brothers

It isn't the mountains ahead to climb that wear you out; it's the pebble in your shoe.

-Muhammad Ali

~

RESEARCH HAS SHOWN THAT THE BEST WAY TO BE HAPPY IS TO MAKE EACH DAY HAPPY.

-DEEPAK CHOPRA

People often say that motivation doesn't last. Well, neither does bathing, that's why we recommend it daily.

-Zig Ziglar

~

If you're still looking for that one person who can change your life, take a look in the mirror.

-Roman Price

If you take responsibility for yourself you will develop a hunger to accomplish your dreams.

-Les Brown

~

No man's knowledge here can go beyond his experience

-John Locke

If someone is going
down the wrong road,
he doesn't need
motivation to speed
him up. What he needs
is education to turn
him around

-Jim Rohn

~

**The habit of being happy
enables one to be freed, or
largely freed, from the
domination of outward
conditions.**

-Robert Louis Stevenson

That some achieve great success is proof to all that others can achieve it as well.

-Abraham Lincoln

~

A friend is a gift you give yourself.

-Robert Louis Stevenson

Because a thing seems difficult for you, do not think it impossible for anyone to accomplish.

-Marcus Aurelius

~

A house divided against itself cannot stand.

-Abraham Lincoln

Everything you are against weakens you. Everything you are for empowers you.

-Wayne Dyer

~

I believe that you should gravitate to people who are doing productive & positive things with their lives.

-Nadia Comaneci

Judgments prevent us from seeing the good that lies beyond appearances.

-Wayne Dyer

~

Money & success don't change people; they merely amplify what is already there.

-Will Smith

Play like you're positive on the
victory, even though they're leading
big now.

-Knute Rockne

~

Take time to gather up the
past so that you will be
able to draw from your
experience & invest them
in the future.

-Jim Rohn

A LEADER IS ONE WHO KNOWS THE WAY-
GOES THE WAY- & SHOWS THE WAY.

-JOHN MAXWELL

~

It's not what you've got;
it's what you use that
makes a difference.

-Zig Ziglar

Formal education will make you a living; self-education will make you a fortune.

-Jim Rohn

~

In the end people are persuaded not by what we say but by what they understand.

-John Maxwell

Help others achieve their dreams & you will achieve yours.

-Les Brown

~

Either you run the day or the day runs you.

-Jim Rohn

I believe that when you work on yourself you are attracted by different, more positive beings.

-Isabelle Adjani

~

Surmounting difficulty is the crucible that forms character.

-Tony Robbins

If you do what you've always done- you'll get what you've always gotten.

-Tony Robbins

~

Decide that you want it more than you are afraid of it.

-Bill Cosby

More people would
learn from their
mistakes if they
weren't so busy
denying them.

-J. Harold Smith

~

**If you fall, fall on your back. If
you can look up you can get up.**

-Les Brown

Goals allow you to control the direction of change in your favor.

-Brian Tracy

~

Don't Doubt Life. Live Life

~Alicia Gross

People are often unreasonable,
illogical and self centered;
Forgive them anyway.

If you are kind, people may
accuse you of selfish, ulterior
motives;
Be kind anyway.

If you are successful, you will
win some false friends and
some true enemies;
Succeed anyway.

If you are honest and frank,
people may cheat you;
Be honest and frank anyway.

What you spend years building, someone could destroy overnight;
Build anyway.

If you find serenity and happiness, they may be jealous;
Be happy anyway.

The good you do today, people will often forget tomorrow;
Do good anyway.

Give the world the best you have, and it may never be enough;
Give the world the best you've got anyway.

-Mother Teresa

Printed in Great Britain
by Amazon.co.uk, Ltd.,
Marston Gate.